International Red Cross

A book about the International Red Cross and Red Crescent Movement

Ralf Perkins

W
FRANKLIN WATTS
LONDON•SYDNEY

This edition 2004 by Franklin Watts
96 Leonard Street, London EC2A 4XD

Franklin Watts Australia
45–51 Huntley Street, Alexandria, NSW 2015

Editor: Rachel Cooke
Designer: Simon Borrough
Picture research: Sue Mennell

Franklin Watts thank the Red Cross Movement for
their co-operation and advice in producing this
book, but would like to make it clear that this is not
a Red Cross publication.

A CIP catalogue record for this book is available
from the British Library.

ISBN   0 7496 5695 6
Dewey classification 361.7

Printed in Malaysia

Picture credits:
Cover images: Topham Picturepoint/
Associated Press (left); Panos Pictures/Zed
Nelson (top right); British Red Cross
Society (bottom left)
Inside: AKG London pp. 4t, 4b; British
Red Cross Society pp. 1, 9, 11, 12l, 12r,
23t, 25, 27t; Corbis pp. 5 (Bill Gentile),
7t (Reuters New Media Inc.), 8t (Joseph
Sohm/ChromoSohm Inc), 24 (Liba
Taylor), 26 (Liba Taylor); International
Committee of the Red Cross pp. 15
(Thierry Gassmann), 19b (Boris Heger),
28t (Till Mayer); International Federation
of Red Cross and Red Crescent
Societies pp. 3, 7b, 10b, 27b (Lars
Schwetije), 28b; Magnum Photos p. 29b
(David Hurn); Popperfoto 13t, 14t;
Popperfoto/Reuters pp. 1r (Rafiqur
Rahman), 2t (Sergei Teterin), 2-3 (Yves
Herman), 6 (Sergei Teterin), 8b (Mona Sharaf),
10t (Yves Herman), 13b (Yuri Tutor), 14-15, 16,
17l (Damir Sagoli), 17r (El Tiempo), 18, 19t (Chor
Sokunthea), 20l (Christian Charisius), 20r (Rafiqur
Rahman), 21 (Henry Romero) 22 (Michael Dalder),
29t (Philippe Wojazer).

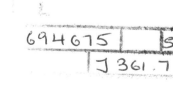

▲ *The emblems of the International Red Cross and Red Crescent Movement.*

The Red Cross provides help for people in need or crisis – whether the crisis be caused by war, disaster, accidents or more day-to-day problems such as ill-health. The Movement (as it is often called) is one of the oldest and largest independent humanitarian organizations in the world.

◀ Henry Dunant, the Red Cross founder.

▶ An early Red Cross volunteer helps the injured in war-torn Paris in 1870.

The Battle of Solferino

The Red Cross began almost 150 years ago when one man told the world about the brutality of war.

On 24 June 1859, the French and Italian armies won a savage battle against the Austrians at Solferino in northern Italy. By nightfall, the armies had gone, but they left behind them over 40,000 dead and injured soldiers.

Henry Dunant, a young Swiss businessman, was shocked by the soldiers' terrible suffering. He gathered together a little group of local women and passing travellers to help. They cared for the wounded, comforted the dying and buried the dead. The helpers came from different countries, but they all worked together. Later Dunant said proudly that they had been 'tutti fratelli' – all brothers.

Problem

Who should you help?

When faced with many injured people, who do you help and who do you treat first? At Solferino, Dunant helped wounded soldiers from both sides. He felt no one should be denied help who needed it, but that the people whose suffering was greatest should be treated first. This idea of impartiality has become a guiding principle of the Red Cross ever since. The Movement helps people because they need it, regardless of their nationality, race, religion or political beliefs.

▼ *A Red Cross worker waves the Red Cross flag during fighting in the civil war in El Salvador in 1989. The protective flag shows that he is neutral and impartial and not involved in the conflict.*

Permanent national relief societies

In 1862 Dunant published *A Memoir of Solferino* revealing the horrors of war. In it Dunant called for permanent relief societies in each country to train and equip volunteers in times of peace to look after soldiers who were wounded in war. These volunteers would be attached to their country's armies and would assist any soldier who needed medical help or comfort.

Several Swiss gentlemen agreed with Dunant's humanitarian aims. At a meeting in Geneva on 17 February 1863, Dunant and four others formed the International Committee for Relief to the Wounded, which later became the International Committee of the Red Cross (ICRC).

The Geneva Conventions

The Red Cross idea quickly won support from other European countries such as Belgium, Denmark and Portugal. At Geneva in 1864, delegates from 12 different countries framed a set of rules about how to treat wounded soldiers and medical workers in war. This became the original Geneva Convention.

No one before had tried to make general international laws about armed conflict or war, now called humanitarian law. The ICRC helped change all this. Since 1864, the Geneva Convention has been revised several times to cover different types of war victim. Today, there are four Geneva Conventions, and the governments of 191 countries have now signed them. If they break these laws, government officials and army commanders can be prosecuted for war crimes.

Checklist

Humanitarian laws

The four Geneva Conventions aim to protect wounded and sick members of the armed forces on land and at sea, prisoners of war and civilians (people not members of the armed forces) in times of war. These are some of their rules:

- It is forbidden to kill or injure an enemy who surrenders.
- The wounded and sick shall be cared for by the people who have captured them.
- Prisoners of war and captured civilians shall be treated with respect. They shall be allowed to communicate with their families.
- It is forbidden to make a deliberate attack on civilians or their property.

▼ *This woman in Grozny, Chechnya, has lost her house in a Russian bombing raid. If this were a deliberate act, it would break one of the Geneva Conventions.*

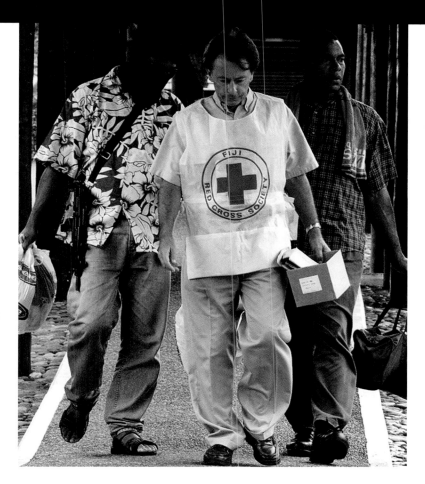

▲ *John Scott, director-general of the Fiji Red Cross, visits the hostages in the Fiji Parliament in May 2000. The rebels holding the hostages were later arrested.*

 ## Spotlight

Being neutral

The Red Cross Movement is neutral – it does not take sides in times of war or other conflict, nor does it involve itself in controversial debates, such as those surrounding politics or religion. In Fiji in 2000, armed rebels took 31 people hostage for eight weeks, including the Fijian prime minister, demanding a change in government. During the crisis, the director-general of the Fiji Red Cross, John Scott, visited the hostages every day, taking essential supplies and exchanging letters. The rebels only let him help the hostages because they knew that the Red Cross was neutral.

 ## Spotlight

The Red Cross and Red Crescent emblems

In 1863 the Red Cross's founding conference chose a red cross on a white background as the emblem for the volunteer medical personnel. This symbol (the reversed colours of the Swiss flag) may have been chosen as a tribute to Switzerland. However, the cross is also seen a Christian symbol and, in fighting between Muslim Turks and Russian Christians in 1876, Turkish Red Cross workers wore a red crescent instead. Governments later recognized the symbol and the two emblems are now used around the world as signs of neutral and impartial care; neither has any religious, national or similar significance.

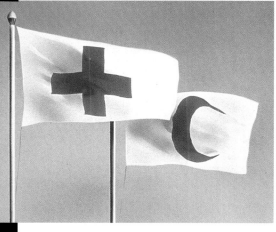

▲ *The Red Cross and Red Crescent flags fly alongside each other. They are special symbols protected by law.*

The Red Cross grows

The drawing up of the first Geneva Convention attracted support around the world. Within 10 years, there were 22 National Red Cross Committees (later Societies) in Europe, including the British Red Cross in 1870 and the Danish in 1876. The American Red Cross was founded in 1881. Now there are 181 recognized National Societies around the world.

All these Societies were founded to provide assistance to the sick and wounded in times of war. However, it soon became apparent that there were other times when their skills could be called up – in times of disaster, such as floods or famine, or in training others to deal with emergency situations.

▶ *An American Red Cross disaster truck, ready to carry aid to people hit by floods, fire and storms.*

▼ *A German Red Cross rescue worker searches for survivors in a collapsed building in Cairo in 1996.*

 Spotlight

Peacetime disaster relief

In September 1881, a forest fire raced across the state of Michigan, killing hundreds of people and leaving thousands homeless. Clara Barton, the founder of the American Red Cross, took building tools, clothes and cash to help the fire's victims. In 1882-3 she helped flood victims in Mississippi, and in 1891 she sent food to starving peasants in Russia.

Today the Red Cross is a vast international Movement, with around 97 million members in 181 different countries. Each part of this Movement is independent from the other, but they are united by shared aims and ideals.

The International Committee of the Red Cross

The International Committee of the Red Cross (ICRC) is the founding body of the organization. It is still based in Geneva but it employs delegates from all around the world. The International Committee is particularly concerned with the protection of people during armed conflict, including civilians and prisoners of war, although it works with the National Societies to achieve its aim. The ICRC has been instrumental in the drawing up and amending of the Geneva Conventions and promotes humanitarian law.

▲ The headquarters of the ICRC in Geneva. Its French name is Comité International de la Croix-Rouge.

Checklist

The different parts of the Red Cross and Red Crescent Movement are:

- The International Committee of the Red Cross (ICRC)
- The International Federation of Red Cross and Red Crescent Societies
- 181 National Red Cross and National Red Crescent Societies

The National Societies

There are 181 recognized National Societies, such as the Japanese Red Cross and the Iranian Red Crescent. To qualify as a member of the Red Cross Movement, a Society must meet certain criteria – for example, each Society must be legally recognized by its country as an independent voluntary aid organization, which provides support to the country's public authorities. This enables the Societies to support their country's army medical services in wartime and the civilian medical and emergency services at all times. However, it also means that a Society can give care to anyone who needs it, regardless of nationality.

▲ Red Cross volunteers assist a spectator who was injured when a stand collapsed at a football match in Brussels.

A range of services

Alongside their emergency role, each National Society provides a range of support services, which vary from country to country. For example, the American Red Cross provides a blood donation service but the British Red Cross does not. Many provide first-aid stations at sporting events, pop concerts and festivals. Often they teach first-aid to schools, social clubs and businesses. They also provide funding and expertise for the Movement internationally.

The International Federation

The National Societies all belong to one big group called the International Federation of Red Cross and Red Crescent Societies. The International Federation co-ordinates disaster relief provided by the different Societies and helps the National Societies to develop their services. In addition, it assists countries who want to set up Societies.

 Spotlight

On 26 December 2003, an earthquake struck the city of Bam in south-eastern Iran, killing more than 41,000 people and leaving another 75,000 without homes. The International Federation of Red Cross and Red Crescent Societies led efforts in Bam to provide health care, clean water, food and psychological support, and established 12 tent camps around the city to house survivors. One amazing rescue story involved a 97-year-old woman, whom Red Cross workers found alive in the rubble, eight days after the earthquake.

▼ After an earthquake in Turkey in 1999, the International Federation worked with the Turkish Red Crescent to provide relief.

Working together

Representatives from the National Societies, the International Federation and the International Committee meet for a conference with the governments of countries who have signed the Geneva Conventions to discuss the principles that unite the Movement and other matters of common humanitarian concern. These conferences usually take place once every four years. At a conference in 1965, the Red Cross and Red Crescent Movement agreed to seven Fundamental Principles which are based on the ideas which formed the Movement and that it still upholds today (see panel).

(see panel)

✓ Checklist

The Fundamental Principles of the Red Cross

Humanity – The Movement aims to prevent and lessen human suffering wherever it may be found.

Impartiality – See page 5.

Neutrality – See page 7.

Independence – The National Societies, while supporting their governments, remain independent.

Voluntary Service – See page 12.

Unity – There can be only one Red Cross or Red Crescent Society in any one country. It must be open to all.

Universality – The Movement is a worldwide one, where all the Societies share equal status and responsibilities.

▲ Delegates from the International Red Cross and Red Crescent Movement meet in Birmingham, England, in 1993.

Who pays for the Red Cross?

The Red Cross needs a large amount of money to carry out its work around the world. In 2002 the International Committee in Geneva spent approximately 820 million Swiss Francs (about £350 million). This does not include the money spent by National Societies.

All of this money is donated, some of it via the National Societies. A lot of it comes from governments and international bodies like the European Union. The Red Cross does not accept donations which would require it to act against its Fundamental Principles. This means, for example, a government that gives money to help refugees cannot demand that the money assists people of only one nationality or race.

Private donations

Private individuals and companies also give money to the Red Cross. Private donations are vital when a disaster strikes. If Armenia suffers an earthquake or Ethiopia faces famine, the Red Cross asks people all over the world for donations to help the victims of that disaster. It runs appeals on television and in newspapers.

Spotlight

World Red Cross and Red Crescent Day
Every year 8 May, Henry Dunant's birthday, is celebrated as World Red Cross and Red Crescent Day. On this day the Red Cross makes a world-wide appeal for donations, and it encourages newspapers and television stations to publicize its work. Red Cross volunteers collect money from the public and people wear a Red Cross badge.

A voluntary workforce

People who work for the Red Cross do so because they want to help others and of their own free will, not because they expect to make money from it. This voluntary service is an important principle of the Red Cross. In the vast majority of cases, it means that the volunteers give their time for free.

However, all sections of the Red Cross have paid employees too. Delegates are the people who work for the international sections of the Movement, although they may be supported financially by the National Societies. These delegates are skilled workers, such as health co-ordinators and engineers, who can be sent to any part of the world to relieve human suffering in wars and disasters.

▲ *Sales of seasonal cards raise money for some National Societies.*

▲ *A Red Cross helper appeals for donations from the public.*

Warfare has changed since Henry Dunant's lifetime. Weapons are deadlier and civilians often suffer in war as much as soldiers do. Through two world wars and many subsequent conflicts, the Red Cross has adapted to these changes but it still provides neutral support to those in need.

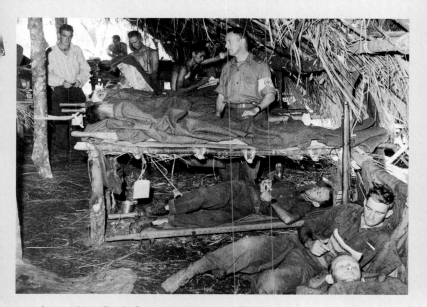

▲ *Australian Red Cross workers staff an emergency medical post for wounded soldiers in New Guinea during World War II.*

Battlefield support

The Red Cross's original war work remains vital. In World War I, Red Cross Societies provided nurses and other staff to treat the injured. Today, when most armies provide their own medical services, the National Societies often support their armies in different ways — helping soldiers remain in contact with their families at home or visiting injured troops in hospital, for example.

▲ *Russian women ask an ICRC worker to help them trace their husbands and sons who are fighting in the Russian conflict in Chechnya.*

 Spotlight

For the past 25 years, an armed group called the Polisario Front has held nearly 2000 Moroccans captive in the western Sahara. Every year ICRC delegates visit these forgotten prisoners, taking them news and family letters and providing medical assistance. In February 2000, 126 elderly and ill prisoners were released. The Front and the Moroccan government used the ICRC as a neutral go-between in the release process.

▲ A British Red Cross worker checks care parcels to be sent to prisoners of war in Korea in 1952.

Prisoners of war

In most conflicts, soldiers and sometimes civilians are taken prisoner on both sides. The Third Geneva Convention recognizes the role of the ICRC as a neutral organization whose representatives must be allowed to visit these prisoners. The ICRC delegates visit prisoners of war and try to put them in touch with their families. They check prisoners have proper food and medical care and that they are not being ill-treated.

▲ The Red Cross Movement provides food for civilians forced to flee their homes during war.

▼ Red Cross nurses give emergency aid to a man wounded in Rwanda's civil war in April 1995.

Protecting civilians

A major part of the Red Cross's wartime work now is helping civilians. When fighting breaks out, the ICRC, working with the National Societies, tries to maintain basic medical supplies, food and water services, so that ordinary people do not die of starvation or disease while the fighting rages around them. It sets up refugee shelters for people who are forced out of their homes. It collects names and photographs of missing people and tries to trace them in enemy prisons, refugee camps or among the dead.

If necessary, the ICRC will supply trained medical teams to assist in local hospitals that cannot cope with the demand on their resources. ICRC surgeons train local doctors to deal with wounds that happen in a war, so that they can take over once the ICRC team has moved on.

When the fighting stops

War leaves behind it many people who suffer long after the fighting has stopped. The victims of war may have physical problems, such as injuries received from a bomb. Sometimes they have emotional problems as well. Red Cross workers help all these people. They organize the rebuilding of hospitals and schools. They provide seeds, fertilizer and equipment so farming can begin again. Counsellors help people to understand the horrible things they have seen in war. Researchers reunite missing people with their families.

▼ *Young refugees from Rwanda in an ICRC truck. They have been separated from their families by civil war.*

Spotlight

Reuniting families

When fighting in the Korean war stopped nearly 50 years ago, many families were divided between North and South Korea. In 2000 the two Korean governments agreed that the two National Red Cross Societies could organize some family reunions. Park Yoon-sung, aged 85, lives in South Korea. The Red Cross escorted him to North Korea to meet his two brothers. 'I never dreamt of this happening,' Park Yoon-sung said. 'I miss my brothers so much.'

The horrors of war

At times of war, people and governments can do terrible things. People's human rights and humanitarian law are often ignored. Some aid organizations speak out publicly against human rights abuses they witness. However, the Red Cross rarely publicly criticizes or condemns any government. The Red Cross in no way ignores violations of human rights or humanitarian law but it expresses its concerns privately. Otherwise, a government may not see the Red Cross as neutral and may stop Red Cross workers helping the people who are suffering.

Problem

Aid for Serbia

From the early 1990s, Serbia was at the centre of a series of conflicts in the former Yugoslavia, fighting in Croatia, Bosnia and Kosovo. The Serb government was severely criticized for its conduct in these wars. Despite this, the ICRC continued to support the Yugoslav (that is, Serbian) Red Cross in its humanitarian aid for Serb civilians and refugees. Some other aid agencies refused this help because of Serbia's human rights record.

▲ In 1999 Kosovan refugees, forced from their homes by Serbs, were helped by the Red Cross Movement.

Awareness of the limits on war

The Red Cross Movement constantly promotes humanitarian principles and rules through its support of the Geneva Conventions (see page 6). Both the ICRC and National Societies publish books and leaflets on the Conventions. Red Cross delegates teach humanitarian law to the armed forces, to the general public and to children. In a civil war, the ICRC will try to ensure that all sides in the conflict are informed of humanitarian law and how it affects them.

▲ Red Cross workers are caught in the middle of fighting between government and rebel troops in Colombia, 2000.

Spotlight

Learning the law

Some national Red Cross Societies, including Russia and Belgium, organize 'trial trials'. Groups of law students come together to practise war crimes trials, with actors playing the accused and experts on hand to give advice. In this way, students learn about humanitarian law and the problems lawyers face when trying to prove a person is guilty of breaking the law or defending such a person.

New technology

By promoting the Geneva Conventions, the ICRC also reminds people that they have a responsibility in choosing what weapons they use. Today, advances in technology mean that ever more terrifying weapons can be invented. In 1998 Dr. Cornelio Sommaruga, the then president of the ICRC, warned that 'international humanitarian law has an essential role to play in sparing humanity the worst consequences of its technical capabilities.'

Checklist

International humanitarian laws ban the use of certain weapons as inhumane. These include:

- Bullets which shatter when they hit a person
- Chemical weapons – e.g. bombs which release poison gas
- Biological weapons – e.g. bombs which release the germs of a deadly disease
- Anti-personnel landmines – devices, buried underground, that explode when someone steps on them
- Laser weapons that are designed to cause permanent blindness.

Problem

Anti-personnel landmines

Although there is a treaty banning these mines, some countries have not yet signed it and many armies still use them. Buried underground, mines stay active for years after a war is over. Every hour, somewhere in the world, three people are killed or maimed by a mine.

▼ An Iranian child lies in hospital, a victim of a chemical attack made by Iraq during the Iran-Iraq war in 1988. The chemicals have burnt his skin and caused severe blistering.

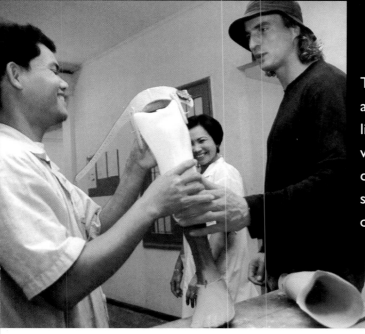

Spotlight

The ICRC has set up over 30 workshops around the world to produce the artificial limbs, crutches and wheelchairs that the victims of landmines need. They try to use cheap, easily-available materials and train local staff, so that the workshops can eventually operate independently.

◀ *Football star David Ginola visits an artificial limb workshop in Cambodia, where many people have been maimed by anti-personnel landmines.*

Problem

New weapons

After the war in Kosovo in 1999, people were at risk not only from mines planted by the Serbian forces but also from some unexploded cluster bombs dropped by the NATO forces. NATO was fighting to protect the Kosovo-Albanians from the Serbs. Cluster bombs are not banned because they should explode on impact, but a small percentage do not.

A cluster bomb looks like a soda-can with a parachute attached – and could be mistaken for a toy. Some Kosovan children have been killed by them. The ICRC trained six people in mine awareness to teach Kosovans about the dangers of mines – they also had to include cluster bombs in their lessons.

▲ *Children in Kosovo read leaflets handed out by the ICRC warning them about the dangers of mines and unexploded bombs left over from the war in 1999.*

 A temporary Red Crescent tent city put up in Turkey for people made homeless by the earthquake in 1999.

Food and shelter

The Red Cross also arranges food and shelter for people who have been made homeless. It sets up hostels in big buildings such as churches and town halls or erects temporary 'tent cities'. When the crisis is over, Red Cross workers help people to return home. If needed, they hand out tools and building materials for people to repair or rebuild their houses. In rural areas they provide seeds and agricultural equipment to allow them to plant new crops.

Problem

Co-ordinating disaster relief

In the floods in Mozambique in February 2000, over 540,000 people lost their homes. Aid poured in: governments sent helicopters and planes, and thousands of aid agencies sent teams to help. 'It was like a circus,' commented one senior aid worker. The Mozambique government initially struggled to co-ordinate the relief. Some tasks were done twice or help given where it wasn't needed. Advised by the Mozambique Red Cross Society, the government set up daily briefings for both the press and aid agencies and ensured that aid agencies acted with their knowledge and consent.

▶ *The Mozambique Red Cross sends out boats to distribute aid and to rescue people trapped by flood waters in March 2000.*

Preparing for the worst

The Red Cross works to lessen the impact of disasters. It provides warning and rescue systems that communities can run by themselves without outside assistance. In the Mozambique floods in 2000, other countries sent helicopters to pluck people to safety from trees and rooftops. But Mozambique cannot afford a permanent rescue system based on helicopters. It is simpler and cheaper to provide small boats to be stored in areas at risk of flooding, so that when floods happen local people can rescue each other.

▶ *A Red Crescent volunteer helps a young child who has lost her home in floods in Bangladesh in 1998.*

 ## Spotlight

Flood alert

In 1991 flooding in Bangladesh killed 140,000 people. In 1998 the floods were worse, but fewer than 1,000 people died. Many lives were saved in 1998 because the International Federation had helped set up a storm warning system. When a storm or cyclone is coming, thousands of volunteers from the Bangladeshi Red Crescent travel up and down the coast using megaphones to tell people to shift to higher ground. The Red Cross Movement also helped build cyclone shelters and artificial hills where people can shelter until a storm is over.

Problem

The poverty trap

Many disasters are caused by humans and they could be avoided. In July 2000, over 150 people living at a rubbish dump in Manila died when a towering mountain of rubbish collapsed in heavy rains, smothering their shanty huts. The victims were some of the poorest people in the Philippines: rubbish pickers who sift through tips looking for items to sell on the streets. The Red Cross always helps in disasters like these, but it also works to provide better living conditions for people.

◀ *Lessons in AIDS awareness given by the Gambia Red Cross to a group of villagers.*

Silent disasters

People give generously to Red Cross appeals for victims of earthquakes, floods and hurricanes. These are big, dramatic disasters that everyone sees on television. But the Red Cross needs money for 'silent disasters' too. These are long-term problems like poverty and disease, which people do not give so much money to fight.

In parts of Africa, the disease AIDS is a 'silent disaster'. Gradually AIDS is killing millions of people. It destroys families and damages national economies. The Red Cross trains local workers to give advice about AIDS. It funds hospitals to care for the sick, and runs orphanages and schools to protect children whose parents have died.

Spotlight

Teaching your friends

The International Federation encourages the National Societies to train young volunteers in AIDS education. Young people will listen to people of their own age more willingly than older authority figures. The Federation supports the Societies by publishing a training manual for young people called *Action with Youth*.

5. Caring for the community

Many people know the Red Cross through the work of the National Societies among their local communities. They provide long and short-term support to those in need.

▼ *Some National Societies offer transport to people who cannot travel by themselves.*

✓ Checklist

The British Red Cross provides the following community services:

- The short-term loan of medical equipment such as wheelchairs
- Transport or escort for elderly and ill people so they can make essential journeys
- Care for people who have just come out of hospital or whose regular carers are away
- Helping people in the UK trace and contact their families overseas who are separated from them by war
- First-aid training and support at public events.

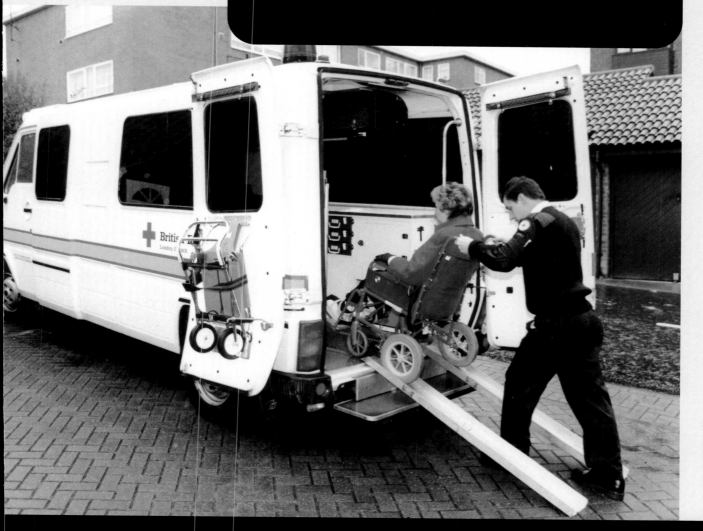

First-aid

Accidents can happen to anyone and anywhere – in the home, at work, in a car. First-aid is the immediate medical care that is given to accident victims, before a doctor or ambulance arrives. It includes stopping heavy bleeding, resuscitating someone who has stopped breathing or cooling burns. Prompt first-aid can mean the difference between an accident victim living or dying.

RELIEF ORGANIZATIONS (OTHER THAN RED CROSS)

FIRST-AID KIT

▲ *The red cross symbol is often misused. A white cross on green is a recognized symbol for first-aid.*

Problem

A sign of protection

The red cross symbol is so often associated with first-aid and medical care that people who are not involved in military medical services or the Movement sometimes use it too. This is against the law in nearly all countries. The Geneva Conventions recognize the symbol as a special one which protects the wounded and sick, and those who have official permission to help them, in times of war. It is important that its effect is not weakened by unauthorized use. The Red Cross Societies work with their governments to stop illegal misuses of the symbol. The situation is similar with the red crescent emblem.

National Red Cross and Red Crescent Societies' volunteers provide first-aid cover at big public events to deal with just such an emergency. They also teach first-aid to anyone who wishes to learn it, including children as young as five. The Red Cross sells first-aid courses and first-aid kits to businesses, schools and sports clubs. The money raised from these sales funds other Red Cross work. Some Societies teach first-aid to children for free.

◀ *A woman learns how to bandage a wound at a first-aid class run by the Red Cross in the Gambia.*

Blood banks

In many countries, although not the UK, the National Red Cross or Red Crescent Society runs a blood donation service or 'blood bank'. The Red Cross encourages healthy members of the public to give some of their blood to help others. The blood is labelled and stored by hospitals to be used when someone needs extra blood during surgery or to replace blood that they may have lost in a car crash or other accident.

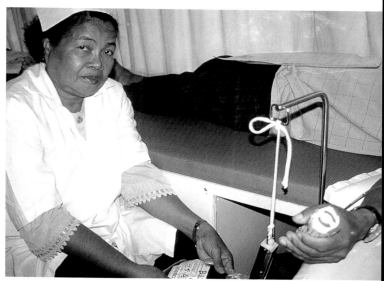

▲ A blood donation service run by the Cambodian Red Cross.

A friend in need

The Red Cross and Red Crescent Societies around the world are active in many areas where people need help. Some provide clothing and emergency supplies for families whose houses have burnt down, for example.

Home visits can be a lifeline for an elderly or ill person. Some Societies provide nurses to make regular visits. Others will help if someone who cares for an ill or elderly relative has to go into hospital. Then a Red Cross volunteer looks after their relative in their absence. Another service Red Cross volunteers take on is to drive patients to and from hospital if they are not well enough to make the journey by themselves.

 Spotlight

Medical research

The Red Cross medical work, both at war and in peacetime, has led some Societies to be involved in medical research. In 1998 the American Red Cross and the United States Army invented a bandage that contains a special blood-clotting agent which stops bleeding quickly. This research is useful not just for work in war zones. The same bandages will save lives in peacetime emergencies, such as car accidents and earthquakes.

◀ A Red Cross volunteer in Bosnia helps an elderly man in his home.

Problem

Care in war

The Sierra Leone Red Cross Society runs health clinics, blood banks and projects within local communities to improve knowledge of health care and risks. From 1991 to 2002 a civil war tore Sierra Leone apart. The Society tried to maintain its everyday care, alongside helping with the wounded and displaced people. Some of its branch offices were looted and, worse still, some of its volunteers killed. As soon as peace returned to its country, the Society began to rebuild its community services.

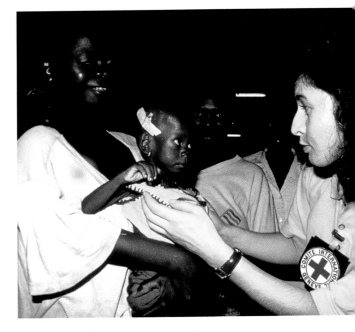

▲ In Sierra Leone, where civil war damaged normal health services, the ICRC helped to run hospitals for civilians.

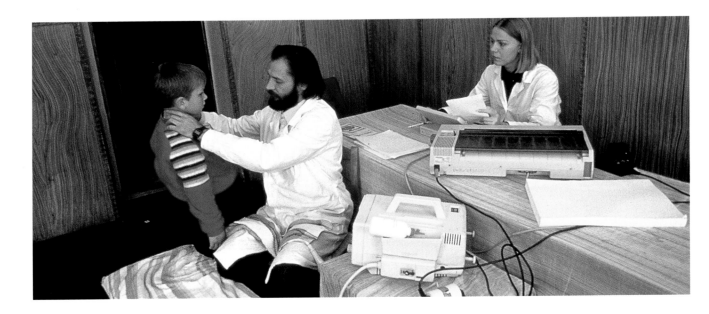

▲ In Belarus a doctor supported by the International Federation of Red Cross and Red Crescent Societies checks a boy for thyroid deficiency.

Helping others

The Red Cross's care and support services improve life for people who are sick, elderly or simply alone. The National Societies can only provide them because of their volunteers – people who give up some of their time to help others in need. The principles that guide the Movement in times of war and disaster are just as important at a community level.

▲ *Two volunteers from the French Red Cross offer help to a homeless man living under a bridge in Paris.*

▼ *Young volunteers learn baby-sitting skills in Arizona, USA. The students are taught by American Red Cross workers how to protect babies from accidents and injuries.*

 Spotlight

The Year of the Volunteer

On 5 December 2000 the United Nations launched their International Year of the Volunteer to recognize and promote the work of volunteers around the world. Speaking at the opening ceremony, Dr. Astrid Heidberg, President of the International Federation of Red Cross and Red Crescent Societies said: 'Everyone likes to make a difference in life... Today we are launching a year to celebrate and promote the hundreds of millions of unselfish women and men, young and old, who give their time and energy to make a difference to the lives of others.'

 Checklist

Red Cross Youth

Anyone can become a Red Cross or Red Crescent volunteer. Societies around the world particularly encourage young people to get involved. Here are just some of the activities of the Red Cross Youth in Denmark:

- holiday camps
- campaigns against racism
- rock concerts
- tree planting in Africa
- playgrounds for children in asylum centres
- first-aid course for young people.

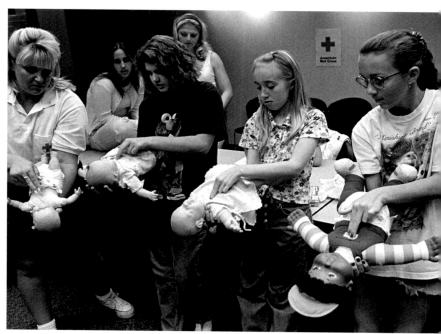

aid
help or assistance; the organized help given to suffering people or poor countries by groups such as the Red Cross and UNICEF

AIDS
Acquired **I**mmune **D**eficiency **S**yndrome, a disease that weakens and kills people by destroying their body's ability to fight off common illnesses

asylum
a place of safety and protection

civil war
a war fought between people living in the same country or of the same nationality

convention
an agreement or contract signed by different countries on an important issue

criteria
standards; conditions or rules that someone has to accept if they wish to join a particular group or society

cyclone
a tornado; a storm with strong circular winds which brings heavy rains with it

diarrhoea
a severe stomach upset that drains the water from a person's body; it can kill babies and young children

humanitarian
concerned with the happiness, safety and welfare of people

impartiality
treating everyone in the same way regardless of their race, nationality or religion

logistics
organizational work, such as providing transport and communication, that makes sure help reaches the people who need it

neutrality
not taking sides in any kind of debate or conflict

shanty huts
unsafe, poor housing made out of flimsy materials such as cardboard, bags and sheets of tin

torture
deliberately to cause intense pain to a person, perhaps as a punishment or to make them reveal a secret

vital
of the greatest importance; essential

war crime
a crime committed in war time which goes against the accepted codes of conduct in war such as the Geneva Conventions

Useful information

International Committee of the Red Cross
Public Information Centre
19 avenue de la Paix
CH 1202 Genève
Switzerland
www.icrc.org

**International Federation of Red Cross
and Red Crescent Societies**
P.O. Box 372
CH 1211 Geneva 19
Switzerland
www.ifrc.org

**To find postal addresses and web sites for
the National Societies:**
www.ifrc.org/address

Some National Society addresses:

American Red Cross
2025 E Street, NW
Washington, DC 20006
USA
www.redcross.org

Australian Red Cross
P.O. Box 196
Carlton South, VIC, 3053
Australia
www.redcross.org.au

British Red Cross
9 Grosvenor Crescent
London SW1X 7EJ
UK
www.redcross.org.uk

Canadian Red Cross Society
170 Metcalfe Street, Suite 300
Ottawa
Ontario K2P 2P2
Canada
www.redcross.ca

Danish Red Cross
P.O. Box 2600
2100 Copenhagen Ö
Denmark
www.redcross.dk

New Zealand Red Cross
P.O. Box 12–140
Thorndon
Wellington 6038
New Zealand
www.redcross.org.nz

**For information on other humanitarian relief
work:**
www.reliefweb.int

United Nations Children's Fund (UNICEF)
www.unicef.org

**United Nations Office for the Coordination
of Humanitarian Affairs**
www.reliefweb.int/ocha_ol/index.html

World Health Organization
www.who.int

Index